A World of Recipes

India

Julie McCulloch

Heinemann
Library

Chicago, Illinois

© 2001 Reed Educational & Professional Publishing
Published by Heinemann Library,
an imprint of Reed Educational & Professional Publishing,
Chicago, IL

Customer Service 888-454-2279

Visit our website at www.heinemannlibrary.com

Designed by Tinstar Design
Illustrations by Nicholas Beresford-Davies
Originated by Dot Gradations
Printed by Wing King Tong in Hong Kong.

05 04 03 02 01
10 9 8 7 6 5 4 3 2 1

Library of Congress Cataloging-in-Publication Data
McCulloch, Julie, 1973-
    India / Julie McCulloch.
        p. cm. -- (A world of recipes)
    Includes bibliographical references and index.
    ISBN 1-58810-085-5 (library binding)
    1. Cookery, India--Juvenile literature. [1. Cookery, India. 2. India--Social life and customs.]
I. McCulloch, Julie, 1973- World of recipes.

TX724.5.I4 M39 2001
641.5954--dc21
                                    00-063273

Acknowledgments
The Publishers would like to thank the following for permission to reproduce photographs:
Robert Harding, p.5; All other photographs by Gareth Boden.
Illustration p.45, US Department of Agriculture/US Department of Health and Human Services.

Cover photographs reproduced with permission of Gareth Boden.

Every effort has been made to contact copyright holders of any material reproduced in this book. Any omissions will be rectified in subsequent printings if notice is given to the Publisher.

Some words in this book are in bold, **like this.** You can find out what they mean by looking in the glossary.

Contents

Key

* easy

** medium

*** difficult

Indian Food

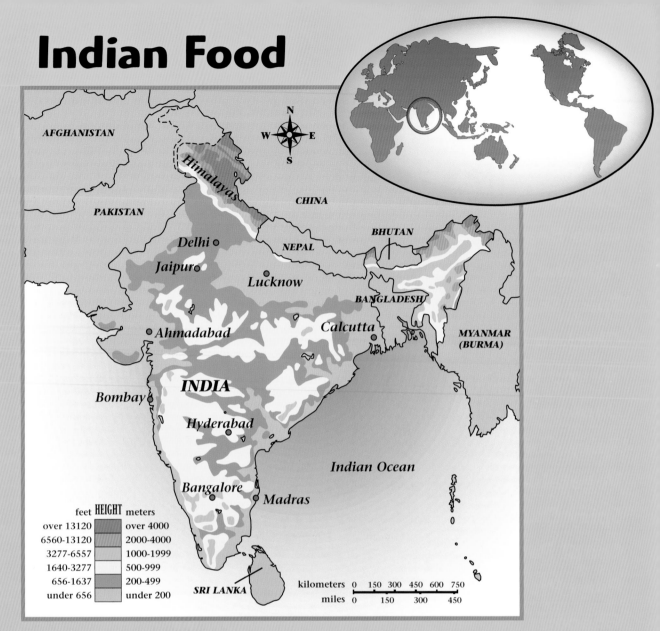

India is a large country in southern Asia. It has a varied climate, with cold mountainous regions in the north and hot, **tropical**, flat areas in the south. Indian cooking can be as different as the land.

In the past

People have lived on the land that is now India for more than five thousand years. The land has been invaded by people from many different countries, who all brought their own cooking traditions with them. During the last 500 years, many European countries fought to control India. Much of India was ruled by the British between 1757 and 1947, when India gained its independence.

In India, religion has the greatest influence on what people eat. Many Indian people are Hindu. This religion is against any form of violence, so many Hindus are **vegetarian.** Some Hindus eat chicken and fish, but eating beef is strictly forbidden, because cows are **sacred** animals. This means that there are a lot of vegetarian dishes in Indian cooking.

Around the country

In northern India, the main crop is wheat, which is ground to make bread. Southern India is very hot and **humid**, and the most important crop is rice. The cooking of southern India is often very spicy. Other crops grown in India include corn, vegetables, bananas, lentils, tea, and coffee.

▲ *The Himalayan mountains in northern India are the highest mountains in the world.*

Indian meals

Indian meals usually consist of several small dishes that are all served at the same time. Hot, spicy dishes are balanced by cool, refreshing ones. Rice or bread is normally served with every meal. Several side dishes are usually served, such as raita (see page 36), a salad, or pickles. Meals are sometimes finished with a dessert.

Indian people usually eat with their fingers. A piece of bread, or a little rice rolled into a ball, is dipped into a sauce or used as a scoop.

Ingredients

chapati

naan

ghee

coconut milk

red lentils

rice

turmeric

ginger

garlic

coconut

cumin

garam masala

ground coriander

chili powder

Bread

Bread often is served as a side dish in India and there are many different types. Chapatis are thin and round and cooked in a hot pan. Naan bread is thick and soft and cooked in an oven. Supermarkets often sell ready-made chapatis and naans.

Coconut

Coconut is used in many dishes, especially in southern India. You may find fresh coconuts in grocery stores, but it is easier to buy it packaged. The recipes in this book use coconut in two different forms—coconut milk, which comes in cans, and dried coconut, which is sold in packets.

Garlic

Garlic is used in many dishes, especially those from northern India. You can buy garlic in the vegetable section of most grocery stores or supermarkets.

Ginger

Fresh ginger is used in many Indian dishes, usually **peeled** and **grated** or finely **chopped.** It is readily available in grocery stores and supermarkets. It is better to use fresh rather than dried ginger, because it has a stronger flavor.

Lentils

Lentils are an important part of many people's diets in India, especially **vegetarians**. They are inexpensive and a good source of **protein**. There are many different types of lentil. The most common type, red lentils, can be found in most grocery stores and supermarkets.

Oil

Most **savory** Indian dishes are cooked in ghee. Ghee is a type of purified butter. It gives a rich, buttery taste to Indian food. Ghee can be difficult to find, so the recipes in this book use vegetable oil.

Rice

Rice is an important ingredient in Indian cooking. There are three main types of rice: short, medium, and long grain. Long-grain rice, especially an Indian rice called basmati, is more suitable for most Indian dishes.

Spices

Spices are plants or seeds with strong flavors that are used to add taste. They are an essential ingredient in many Indian dishes. Some of the most common spices are cumin, turmeric, coriander, garam masala, and chili powder. See page 11 for more about coriander and page 27 for garam masala. You only need to use small amounts of spices. Chili powder can be very hot, so you may prefer to use less or leave it out if you don't like food that is too spicy. Most of these spices can be found in supermarkets.

Before You Begin

Kitchen rules

There are a few basic rules you should always follow when you cook:

- Ask an adult if you can use the kitchen.
- Some cooking processes, especially those involving hot water or oil, can be dangerous. When you see this sign, take extra care or ask an adult to help.
- Wash your hands before you begin.
- Wear an apron to protect your clothes. Tie back long hair.
- Be very careful when using sharp knives.
- Never leave pan handles sticking out—it could be dangerous if you bump into them.
- Always wear oven mitts when lifting things in and out of the oven.
- Wash fruits and vegetables before using them.

How long will it take?

Some of the recipes in this book are quick and easy and some are more difficult and take longer. The strip across the top of the right-hand page of each recipe tells you how long it takes to cook the dish from start to finish. It also shows how difficult each dish is to make: * (easy), ** (medium) or *** (difficult).

Quantities and measurements

You can see how many people each recipe will serve at the top of the right-hand page, too. Most of the recipes in this book make enough to feed two people. A few of the recipes make enough for four. You can multiply or divide the quantities if you want to cook for more or fewer people.

Ingredients for recipes can be measured in two ways. Imperial measurements use cups, ounces, and fluid ounces. Metric measurements use grams and milliliters.

In the recipes you will see the following abbreviations:

tbsp = tablespoon   oz = ounce
tsp = teaspoon   lb = pound
ml = milliliters   cm = centimeters
g = gram

Utensils

To cook the recipes in this book, you will need these utensils as well as kitchen essentials, such as spoons, plates, and bowls:

- cutting board
- colander
- spatula
- food processor or blender
- frying pan

- grater
- measuring cup
- rolling pin
- saucepan with lid
- set of measuring spoons
- sharp knife

(!) Whenever you use kitchen knives, be very careful.

9

Lima Beans with Raisins

Beans are used in many Indian dishes and are a very good source of **protein**. This simple bean dish can be served as an appetizer or as a side dish to a main course.

What you need

1 tbsp fresh cilantro leaves

1 tbsp vegetable oil

1 14-oz (400 g) can lima beans

$1/4$ tsp turmeric

$1/4$ tsp chili powder (optional)

2 tbsp raisins

1 tsp sugar

1 tbsp lemon juice

What you do

1 Finely **chop** the cilantro.

2 **Drain** the liquid from the lima beans by emptying them into a colander.

3 Heat the oil in a frying pan over medium heat.

4 Add the lima beans and cook for 1 minute.

5 Turn the heat down to low. Add the turmeric, chili powder (if you are using it), raisins, sugar, and lemon juice. Cook for another 5 minutes.

6 Add 2 tbsp water and **simmer** for 5 minutes.

7 Sprinkle the chopped cilantro over the beans and raisins before serving.

CORIANDER

Coriander is used in two forms in Indian food. Fresh coriander leaves, an herb, are more commonly called cilantro. Ground coriander seeds are a spice. Cilantro has a strong, fresh taste. It is used for its flavor, to add decoration, and for the bright-green color it gives to sauces. For the recipes in this book, you need about a tablespoonful of leaves.

Ground coriander is made from the crushed seeds of the coriander plant. Ground coriander is added to many Indian dishes and adds a strong, slightly lemony taste.

Fish and Coconut Soup

Savory Indian dishes are not traditionally divided into appetizers or main courses. Several small dishes are usually served all at the same time. This soup would be just one of them.

You can use any kind of white fish you like. Try to find skinless fish fillets. If you use frozen fish, take it out of the freezer and put it into the refrigerator to **defrost** for at least 12 hours before you want to use it.

What you need

1/2 onion
1 clove garlic
1 small piece fresh ginger, 3/4 in. (2 cm) long
2 skinless fish fillets
1 tbsp vegetable oil
1 tsp turmeric
1/4 tsp chili powder (optional)
1 14-oz (400-ml) can coconut milk
1 tbsp lemon juice

What you do

1 **Peel** the onion and finely **chop** it.

2 Peel the garlic clove and ginger and finely chop them.

3 Cut the fish fillets into small pieces.

4 Heat the oil in a saucepan over medium heat. Add the onion, garlic, ginger, turmeric, and chili powder (if you are using it) and **fry** for 5 minutes.

5 Add the coconut milk and bring the mixture to a **boil**.

6 Add the fish pieces and lemon juice. Turn the heat down to medium and **simmer** the soup for 10 minutes.

Spicy Scrambled Eggs

The Parsi people, who live in western India, originally came from the land that is now Iran. When they arrived in India, they brought with them many egg dishes, such as this recipe for scrambled eggs. In India this dish is eaten for breakfast, as a snack, or for supper.

What you need

1 small piece fresh ginger,
   about 3/4 in. (2 cm) long
1 clove garlic
1/2 onion
1 tbsp fresh cilantro leaves
3 eggs
1 tbsp vegetable oil
1/2 tsp chili powder (optional)
1/4 tsp turmeric

What you do

1 **Peel** the ginger and garlic and finely **chop** them.

2 Peel the onion and finely chop it.

3 Finely chop the cilantro leaves.

4 Crack the eggs into a small bowl. **Beat** them with a fork or whisk until the yolk and white are mixed.

⚠ 5 Heat the oil in a saucepan over medium heat. Add the ginger, garlic, onion, chili powder (if you are using it), and turmeric, and fry for 5 minutes.

6 Add the beaten eggs and chopped cilantro. Cook for 5 minutes, stirring often with a wooden spoon, until the eggs start to become solid. Serve immediately.

Chicken Bhuna

Bhuna, which also can be spelled "bhoona," means **fried.** Bhuna dishes are made from fried onions and spices. When coconut is added to this mixture, it makes a rich, creamy sauce.

What you need

2 boneless, skinless chicken breasts
1 onion
1 clove garlic
3 tomatoes
1 tbsp vegetable oil
1/2 tsp garam masala
1/2 tsp ground coriander
1/2 tsp chili powder (optional)
1/2 tsp turmeric
1 oz (25 g) dried coconut

What you do

1 Cut the chicken breasts into bite-size pieces.

2 **Peel** the onion and garlic and finely **chop** them.

3 Chop the tomatoes into small pieces.

(!) 4 Heat the oil in a saucepan over medium heat. Add the chopped onion and garlic, garam masala, coriander, chili powder (if you are using it), and turmeric. Fry for 5 minutes.

5 Add the chicken pieces and chopped tomatoes. Cook the mixture for 20 minutes.

6 While the bhuna is cooking, sprinkle the dried coconut over it. Serve the bhuna with plain, boiled rice.

PLAIN, BOILED RICE

This recipe makes enough plain, boiled rice for two people:
1. Put 1 cup (200 g) of rice into a saucepan.
2. Add 2 cups (500 ml) of water.
3. Bring to a boil, then **simmer** for 20 minutes, stirring occasionally, until the rice has soaked up all the water.

Shrimp Patia

Patia is a sweet and sour dish. The honey gives the sweet taste, and the vinegar the sour taste. Serve with the plain, boiled rice shown on page 17 or with the pilau rice recipe on page 30.

What you need

1/2 onion
1 clove garlic
1 small piece fresh ginger, about 3/4 in. long
1 tbsp vegetable oil
1/2 tsp cumin
1/2 tsp turmeric
1/2 tsp ground coriander
1 tsp paprika
2 tbsp plain yogurt
1 tbsp honey
2 tsp vinegar
2/3 cup (300 g) cooked peeled shrimp
1 tbsp fresh cilantro leaves

What you do

1 **Peel** the onion and finely **chop** it.

2 Peel the garlic and ginger and finely chop them.

3 Heat the oil in a saucepan over medium heat. Add the onion, garlic, ginger, cumin, turmeric, ground coriander, and paprika, and fry for 5 minutes.

4 Reduce the heat and add the yogurt, honey, and vinegar. **Simmer** for 5 minutes.

5 Add the shrimp and simmer the mixture for another 5 minutes.

6 Finely chop the fresh cilantro leaves and sprinkle them over your patia.

TURMERIC AND SAFFRON

Turmeric is a spice used in many Indian dishes to give a unique taste and a bright-yellow color. It is sometimes used as a substitute for saffron, another spice that colors food yellow. Saffron is made from the center of crocus flowers and is very expensive.

Banana Curry

This fruity curry has a sweet, spicy taste. Unripe bananas, which are still slightly green, work best in this dish.

What you need

1 small piece fresh ginger, 3/4 in. (2 cm) long
2 bananas
1 tbsp vegetable oil
1/2 tsp garam masala
1/2 tsp cumin
1/4 tsp chili powder (optional)
1/2 tsp turmeric
1 cup (200 ml) plain yogurt
1 tbsp lemon juice

What you do

1 **Peel** the ginger and finely **chop** it.

2 Peel the bananas and **slice** them about 1/2 in. thick.

3 Heat the oil in a saucepan over medium heat. Add the chopped ginger, garam masala, cumin, chili powder (if you are using it), and turmeric and fry for about 3 minutes.

4 Add the banana slices and stir them into the spices until they are well coated.

5 Reduce the heat and add the yogurt and lemon juice. **Simmer** the curry for 10 minutes.

WHAT IS A CURRY

The word *curry* is used to describe any spicy Indian dish. Indian people don't use the word, and no one knows for sure where the word came from. One theory is that *curry* may have come from the Indian word *karahi,* which is a type of frying pan used all over India for cooking spices.

Spicy Chickpeas

This is a very filling **vegetarian** dish. Like beans and lentils, chickpeas are an important source of **protein.** You can eat this dish the Indian way, by tearing off pieces of chapati, the bread on page 32, and using them to scoop up the chickpeas.

What you need

1 clove garlic
1 onion
2 tomatoes
1/2 cup (125 g) canned chickpeas
1/4 tsp chili powder (optional)
1 tbsp vegetable oil
1/4 tsp ground coriander (see page 11)
1/2 tsp garam masala
1/2 tsp turmeric
1 tbsp lemon juice

What you do

1 **Peel** the garlic and onion and finely **chop** them.

2 Chop the tomatoes into small pieces.

3 **Drain** the liquid from the chickpeas by emptying the can into a colander.

(!) **4** Heat the oil in a saucepan over medium heat. Add the chopped garlic and onion, chili powder (if you are using it), coriander, garam masala, and turmeric and fry for 5 minutes.

5 Add the chopped tomatoes, drained chickpeas, and lemon juice. Cook for 10 minutes.

LUCKY CHICKPEAS

Chickpeas are known as *channa* in India. Many Hindus eat channa on Fridays, because they believe this will bring them good luck.

Vegetable Biryani

A biryani is a dish made of rice with other ingredients added to it. It makes a filling main course.

What you need

1/2 medium onion
1 clove garlic
1/2 carrot
1 medium zucchini
1 vegetable **bouillon cube**
1 tbsp vegetable oil
1 tsp ground cinnamon
1/2 tsp turmeric
1/2 tsp garam masala
1/2 cup (100 g) rice
1/2 cup (60 g) frozen
  peas, **thawed**
1/2 cup (60 g) chopped,
mixed nuts
1/4 cup (25 g) raisins

What you do

1 **Peel** the onion and garlic and finely **chop** them.

2 Wash the carrot, then cut it into small pieces.

3 Cut off the top and bottom of the zucchini. **Slice** one half of the rest and cut each slice into four pieces.

4 Put 2 cups (500 ml) of water into a saucepan. Bring it to a **boil.** Drop the bouillon cube into the water. Stir until it **dissolves.** Put the **stock** aside.

5 Heat the oil in a saucepan over medium heat. Add the chopped onion and spices, and fry for about 3 minutes.

6 Add the rice and fry for another 5 minutes, stirring from time to time.

7 Add the chopped carrot and zucchini, frozen peas, and stock. Stir well, then reduce the heat to low and **cover** the pan.

8 **Simmer** the mixture for about 20 minutes, stirring from time to time, until all the liquid has been soaked up and the rice is soft.

9 Stir in the chopped nuts and raisins.

MORE BIRYANIS

There are many different variations on the basic biryani. You can make a meat biryani by adding some chopped cooked chicken or a fish biryani by adding cooked shrimp or fish.

Spicy Okra

Okra is a vegetable that grows in many parts of India. It also is known as *bindi* or ladies' fingers. Okra does not have a very strong flavor, but it is excellent at picking up the taste of spices in a dish. When you cook okra, you will see that it produces a lot of sticky "threads." This is perfectly normal! If you can't find okra, try making this dish with eggplant instead. Chop an eggplant into small cubes, then cook it in the same way as the okra.

What you need

1 onion
2 cloves garlic
2 tomatoes
1/2 lb (250 g) okra
1 tbsp vegetable oil
1 tsp ground coriander
1/2 tsp turmeric
1 tsp garam masala

What you do

1 **Peel** the onion and garlic and finely **chop** them.

2 Chop the tomatoes into pieces.

3 Cut the tops and bottoms off the okra and throw them away. **Slice** the okra into 1/2-in. (1 cm) pieces.

4 Heat the oil in a saucepan over medium heat. Add the chopped onion and garlic, coriander, turmeric, and garam masala and fry for 5 minutes.

5 Reduce the heat and add the okra slices and chopped tomatoes. **Simmer** the mixture for 10 minutes.

GARAM MASALA

Garam masala means "hot mixture." It is a mixture of spices that is added to many Indian dishes to add flavor. You can buy ready-mixed garam masala in jars or boxes, but most Indian cooks make their own. It is made by **toasting** black peppercorns, cinnamon, cloves, coriander, and cumin in a frying pan without oil, then **grinding** the toasted spices into a fine powder.

Lentil Patties

More than 60 varieties of lentils are grown in India. The most common are red lentils. Other types of lentils also can be used in this dish. Read the label to see if the lentils need to be soaked before using them.

What you need

2 green onions
1 tbsp fresh cilantro leaves
3/4 cup (125 g) lentils
1/4 tsp chili powder (optional)
1/2 tsp turmeric
3 tbsp white flour
2 tbsp vegetable oil

What you do

1 Cut the tops and bottoms off the green onions and finely **chop** the rest.

2 Finely chop the cilantro leaves.

3 Put the lentils into a saucepan with 1 cup (200 ml) of water. Bring the water to a **boil**, then reduce the heat. **Cover** the pan and **simmer** the lentils for about 20 minutes, until they have soaked up all the water.

4 Add the chopped green onions and cilantro, chili powder (if you are using it), turmeric, and flour. Mix everything together well.

5 Divide the lentil mixture into six pieces. Rub a bit of oil onto your hands so the mixture will not stick, then form each piece into a ball. Flatten each ball into a patty.

6 Heat the rest of the oil in a nonstick frying pan over medium heat. Carefully place the lentil patties into the pan.

7 Cook the patties on one side for 10 minutes, then turn them over with a spatula and cook them on the other side for another 10 minutes.

Pilau Rice with Fruit and Nuts

This rice dish can be a main course or a side dish. Fruits and nuts help to balance the spiciness of dishes such as spicy okra (page 26), shrimp patia (page 18), or chicken bhuna (page 16).

What you need

1 vegetable **bouillon cube**
1 medium onion
1 tbsp vegetable oil
1 tsp ground coriander
1/2 tsp ground cumin
2 tbsp raisins
1/3 cup (50 g) canned pineapple chunks
2 tbsp cashew nuts
3/4 cup (140 g) rice

What you do

1 Pour 2 cups (500 ml) of water into a pan and bring it to a **boil.** Drop the bouillon cube into the water and stir until it **dissolves.** Put the **stock** aside.

2 **Peel** the onion and finely **chop** half of it.

(!) **3** Heat the oil in a saucepan over medium heat. Add the chopped onion, coriander, and cumin and fry for 5 minutes.

4 Add the raisins and pineapple and fry for another 5 minutes.

5 Add the cashew nuts, vegetable stock, and rice and bring the mixture to a boil.

6 Reduce the heat to low. **Cover** the pan and **simmer** for about 20 minutes, stirring from time to time to keep the rice from sticking to the pan, until all the liquid has been soaked up and the rice is soft.

CASHEW NUTS

Cashew trees are common in India. Their nuts, known as cashew nuts, are used in a lot of Indian dishes. They can be added whole, as in this dish, or ground up to make a type of flour that is used to thicken sauces.

Chapatis

Chapatis are soft, flat circles of bread. They are eaten with many different Indian dishes and often are used as a scoop to pick up food.

What you need

1 1/4 cup (140 g) white flour

1/2 tsp salt

What you do

1 Put the salt and 1 cup (100 g) of the flour into a bowl.

2 Gradually stir in 1/2 cup (100 ml) of water. Mix well until the mixture forms a dough.

3 Sprinkle the rest of the flour onto a clean surface. Turn the dough out of the bowl and **knead** it for

 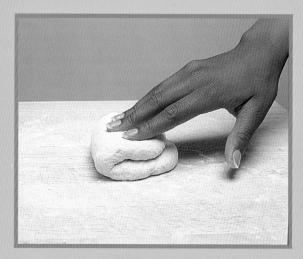

about 10 minutes, until it is smooth.

4 Divide the dough into six pieces. With a rolling pin, roll out each piece of dough into a thin circle.

5 Heat a nonstick frying pan over medium heat. Do not add any oil. Place one chapati in the pan.

6 Cook the chapati for about 1 minute, until it has brown patches. Turn it over with a spatula and cook the other side for another minute.

7 Cook the rest of the chapatis in the same way.

INDIAN BREADS

Bread is very popular in India. It can be **baked**, fried, or **grilled.** In many cities, you can find bread sellers called *tandoor wallahs.* They set up portable ovens, or tandoors, on street corners and use them to cook bread for the nearby households.

Corn and Coconut Salad

This salad makes an ideal side dish to a spicy main course. It is quick and easy to make, too.

What you need

3/4 cup (100 g) frozen corn
1 tbsp fresh cilantro leaves
1 cup (100 g) dried coconut
2 tbsp lemon juice
1/4 tsp chili powder (optional)

What you do

1 Put the corn into a saucepan. Add enough water to cover it.

2 Bring the water to a **boil**, then reduce the heat to a **simmer**. Simmer the corn for 5 minutes.

3 **Drain** the water from the corn by emptying the pan into a colander.

4 Run cold water over the corn to cool it, then put it into a salad bowl.

5 **Chop** the cilantro leaves, then add them to the salad bowl.

6 Add the dried coconut, lemon juice, and chili powder (if you are using it) to the salad bowl.

7 Mix everything together well.

CORN

Corn is grown all over India. The grains of the corn are often used as a vegetable, as in this dish. They also can be ground into a type of flour, which is used to make bread and thicken sauces.

Raita

Because many Indian dishes are spicy, they are often accompanied by light, fresh dishes such as raita. The main ingredient in raita is yogurt, which can be mixed with ingredients such as vegetables and herbs.

What you need

$1/2$ cup (100 ml)
   plain yogurt
1 tbsp fresh cilantro
   leaves
$1/4$ tsp nutmeg

What you do

1 Put the yogurt into a small bowl.

2 Finely **chop** the cilantro and add it to the yogurt.

3 Add the nutmeg.

4 Mix everything together well.

Raisin raita

Mixed raita

Plain raita

Mint raita

Potato raita

MORE RAITA RECIPES

There are many different variations to the basic raita.
You may like to try some of them.

Mixed raita

Chop a 1 1/4-in. long piece of cucumber, 1/2 onion, and a
tomato into small pieces. Add them to the basic raita.

Raisin raita

Add 1 tbsp golden raisins to the basic raita.

Mint raita

Finely chop 1 tbsp fresh mint leaves.
Add it to the basic raita.

Potato raita

Wash a medium potato, then chop it into small pieces.
Boil the potato pieces in enough water to cover them for
5 minutes. **Drain** the potatoes, then add them to
the basic raita.

Banana Fritters

The bananas and sugar in this dish make an ideal change of taste from the spicy, **savory** Indian main courses.

What you need

2 eggs
1 tbsp sugar
2 tbsp white flour
2/3 cup (150 ml) milk
3 bananas
1 tbsp vegetable oil

What you do

1 Crack the eggs into a large bowl. **Beat** them with a fork or whisk until the yolk and white are mixed.

2 Add the sugar, flour, and milk. Mix everything together well.

3 **Peel** the bananas and **slice** them. Add the slices to the bowl.

(!) 4 Heat the oil in a frying pan over medium heat. Carefully spoon all the banana fritter mixture into the frying pan.

5 Gently **fry** the fritter for 5 minutes, then turn it over with a spatula and cook the other side for another 5 minutes.

6 Slide the fritter onto a plate and cut it into four pieces.

EXPENSIVE DECORATION

Indian desserts are sometimes decorated with tissue-thin sheets of real silver called *varaq*. The silver may be wrapped around nuts, which are then placed on top of the food, or simply draped over the dish. On very special occasions, pure gold may be used instead!

Kulfi

Kulfi is a type of Indian ice cream. It makes a creamy, cool end to a meal. People have made ice cream in India for centuries. There is an Indian legend that the emperors sent runners up into the Himalayan mountains to fetch huge chunks of ice to make ice cream. But by the time the runner arrived back at the palace, the ice had always melted!

Take the kulfi out of the freezer at least half an hour before you want to eat it to give it time to soften.

What you need

¹/₄ cup (25 g) shelled, unsalted pistachio nuts

¹/₂ cup (100 ml) evaporated milk

1 cup (200 ml) heavy cream

2 tbsp sugar

1 tsp vanilla extract

What you do

1 **Chop** the pistachio nuts into tiny pieces with a sharp knife.

2 Pour the evaporated milk and cream into a saucepan. Bring them to a **boil**.

3 Add the sugar and vanilla extract, then reduce the heat to low.

4 **Simmer** the mixture for 15 minutes, stirring often. The mixture will gradually thicken.

5 Empty the mixture into a bowl, add the chopped pistachio nuts, and allow to cool.

6 When the mixture has cooled, put the bowl in the freezer.

7 Allow the kulfi to freeze for at least 5 hours.

KULFI MOLDS

In India, kulfi is usually frozen in small, metal, cone-shaped molds to give it a distinctive shape.

Lassi

Lassi is a traditional Indian drink that is served with a meal. Lassi comes in both **savory** and sweet versions. The savory version is called *lassi namkeen,* and the sweet version is called *lassi meethi.*

What you need

Savory lassi:
6 ice cubes
3/4 cup (150 ml)
   plain yogurt
3/4 cup (150 ml) milk
3/4 tsp ground cumin

Sweet lassi:
6 ice cubes
1 mango
3/4 cup (150 ml) plain
   yogurt
3/4 cup (150 ml) milk
2 tsp sugar

What you do

Savory lassi

1 Put the ice cubes in a plastic bag and crush them with a rolling pin.

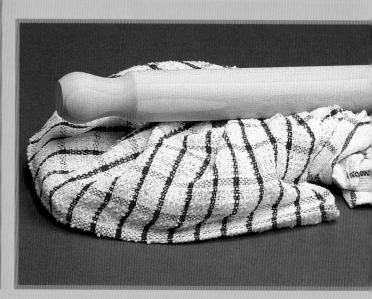

2 Put all the other ingredients into a blender or food processor.

3 **Blend** everything together on the highest setting.

4 Put the crushed ice into two glasses.

5 Pour the lassi over the ice.

Sweet lassi

1 Put the ice cubes in a plastic bag and crush them with a rolling pin.

2 **Peel** the mango and remove the pit from the middle.

3 Cut the mango into pieces.

4 Put the mango pieces, yogurt, milk, and sugar into a blender or food processor.

5 Blend everything together on the highest setting.

6 Put the crushed ice into two glasses.

7 Pour the lassi over the ice.

BUTTERMILK

Another popular drink in India is buttermilk. Buttermilk is the milky liquid that is left when cream is made into butter. In India, people often drink buttermilk with breakfast or lunch.

More Books

Cookbooks

Denny, Roz. *A Taste of India*. Austin, Tex.: Raintree Steck-Vaughn, 1994

Madavan, Vijay. *Cooking the Indian Way*. Minneapolis, Minn.: Lerner Publications, 1985.

Wolfe, Robert. *Vegetarian Cooking Around the World*. Minneapolis, Minn.: Lerner Publications, 1993. An older reader can help you with this book.

Books About India

Barker, Amanda. *India*. Chicago, Ill.: Heinemann Library, 1996.

Landau, Elaine. *India*. Danbury, Conn.: Children's Press, 2000.

Comparing Weights and Measures

3 teaspoons = 1 tablespoon	1 tablespoon = 1/2 fluid ounce	1 teaspoon = 5 milliliters
4 tablespoons = 1/4 cup	1 cup = 8 fluid ounces	1 tablespoon = 15 milliliters
5 1/3 tablespoons = 1/3 cup	1 cup = 1/2 pint	1 cup = 240 milliliters
8 tablespoons = 1/2 cup	2 cups = 1 pint	1 quart = 1 liter
10 2/3 tablespoons = 2/3 cup	4 cups = 1 quart	1 ounce = 28 grams
12 tablespoons = 3/4 cup	2 pints = 1 quart	1 pound = 454 grams
16 tablespoons = 1 cup	4 quarts = 1 gallon	

Healthy Eating

This diagram shows which foods you should eat to stay healthy. You should eat 6–11 servings a day of foods from the bottom of the pyramid. Eat 2–4 servings of fruits and 3–5 servings of vegetables a day. You should also eat 2–3 servings from the milk group and 2–3 servings from the meat group. Eat only a few of the foods from the top of the pyramid.

In India, most meals include rice, chapatis, or naan bread, which all belong to the bread group. Chicken and fish are sometimes used in Indian cooking, but many people are vegetarian and get their **protein** from beans and lentils instead. Yogurt is a popular dairy product. Many fruits and vegetables are used in Indian cooking. Fats, oils, and sweets are also part of Indian cooking.

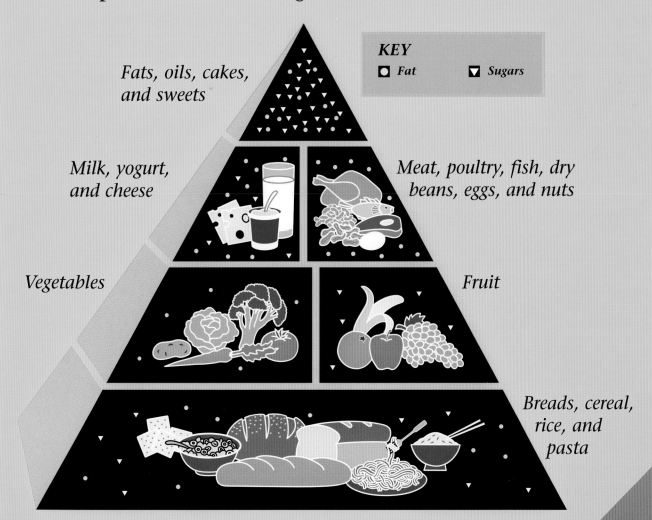

Fats, oils, cakes, and sweets

KEY
◻ *Fat*   ▽ *Sugars*

Milk, yogurt, and cheese

Meat, poultry, fish, dry beans, eggs, and nuts

Vegetables

Fruit

Breads, cereal, rice, and pasta

Glossary

bake to cook something in the oven

beat to mix something together strongly, for example egg yolks and whites

blend to mix ingredients together in a blender or food processor

boil to cook a liquid on the stove until it bubbles and steams strongly

bouillon cube small cube of powdered meat or vegetable powder used to make a base for soups or sauces

chop to cut something into small pieces with a knife

cover to put a lid on a pan or foil over a dish

defrost to allow something that is frozen to reach room temperature

dissolve to stir something, such as sugar, until it disappears into a liquid

drain to remove liquid from a pan or can of food

fry to cook something by placing it in hot oil or fat

grate to shred something by rubbing it back and forth over a utensil that has a rough surface

grill to cook something over an open flame

grind to crush something, such as the seed of a spice plant, until it is a powder

humid climate that is hot and wet

knead to mix ingredients into a smooth dough

peel to remove the skin of a fruit or vegetable

protein body-building material found in some foods, such as beans, eggs, and meat

sacred holy or respected because of religious laws

savory dish that is not sweet

simmer to cook a liquid on the stovetop just under a boil

slice to cut something into thin, flat pieces

stock broth made by slowly cooking meat or vegetables in water or by dissolving a cube of powdered meat flavoring in water

thaw to allow something that has been frozen to come to room temperature

toast to cook something in a pan without any oil in it

tropical place where the weather is hot and wet

vegetarian diet that usually does not include meat or fish, and that sometimes does not include eggs or dairy products; person who follows such a diet

Index